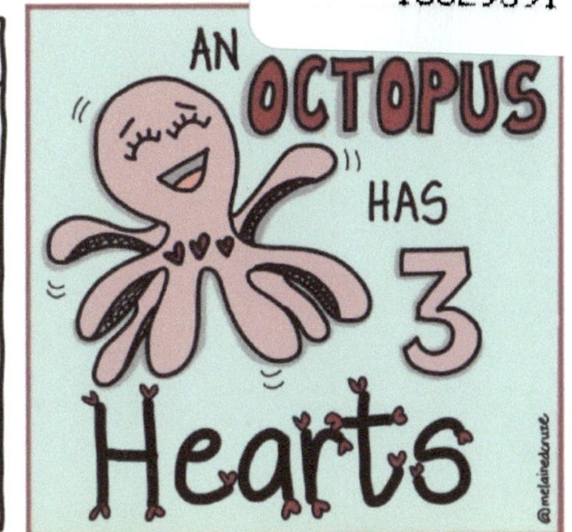

FIFTY FUN FACTS FULLY ILLUSTRATED

Melaine D'Cruze

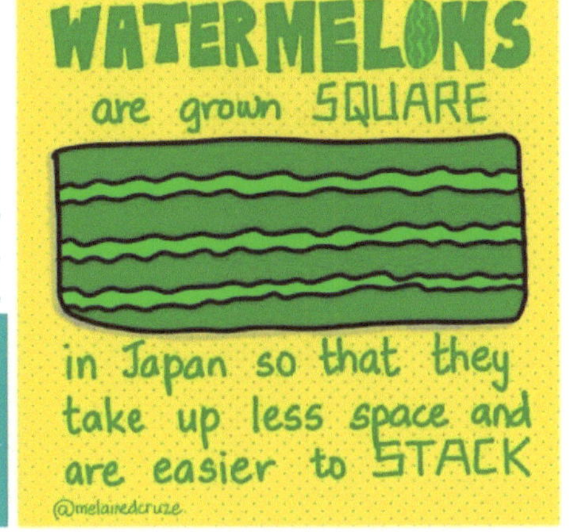

Fifty Fun Facts Fully Illustrated

Melaine D'Cruze

DEDICATED TO
BRADLEY & RILEY
&
ALL THE KIDS WITH
101 QUESTIONS FOR
THEIR PARENTS
STAY CURIOUS!
@melainedcruze

ACKNOWLEDGMENTS

I am eternally grateful to the following people who have inspired me to publish this book: Christopher, Bradley and Riley D'Cruze; Peter, May, Janelle and Brendon Dias; all my family and friends for their encouragement and support; Diane Bleck and the Doodle Institute students and friends; Mike Lowery and the other course facilitators at Sketchbook Skool; and everyone else who believes in the power of putting a pen to paper and dreaming…

HONEY

is the only food that does not SPOIL.

@melainedcruze

BUTTERFLIES USED
to be called
O...
IDENTITY
CRISIS!
FLUTTERBYS
@melainedcruze

SCIENTISTS ESTIMATE THAT THERE ARE 15 MILLION STARS FOR EVERY 1 PERSON ON EARTH
WE ARE OUTNUMBERED!
@melainedcruze

ALL I CAN THINK OF IS
LOVE
@melainedcruze

It was widely believed in the MIDDLE AGES that the

HEART was the centre of HUMAN INTELLIGENCE

1 BLUE WHALE = 40 ELEPHANTS
@melainedcruze

ILLUSTRATE A FUN FACT

@melainedcruze

AN OCTOPUS HAS
3
Hearts
@melainedcruze

@melainedcruze
GOLF
is the only sport
that has been played
ON THE MOON

22,000 men took 20 YEARS to build the TAJ MAHAL
THAT'S A LOT OF MANPOWER!
@melainedcruze

I WAS INVENTED IN
NEW YORK IN 1857
@melainedcruze

The word 'CHECKMATE' in chess comes from the Persian phrase, 'SHAH MAT,' which means 'THE KING IS DEAD'
@melainedcruze

ILLUSTRATE A FUN FACT

More than a 1000 new INSECTS are discovered every year.
@melainedcruze

CANDLES burn better
when they are FROZEN
@melainedcruze

An apple, potato & onion all taste SWEET if you eat them with your NOSE PLUGGED
@melainedcruze

@melainedcruze
BIGGER RAINDROPS MAKE
BRIGHTER RAINBOWS

contain more VITAMIN-C than

ILLUSTRATE A FUN FACT

MOST
LIPSTICKS
CONTAIN
FISH
SCALES
@melainedcraze

PTERONOPHOBIA

is the fear of being tickled by FEATHERS !!!

The OLDEST fish in captivity lived to **88** years of age.

@melainedcruze

WATERMELONS
are grown SQUARE
in Japan so that they
take up less space and
are easier to STACK
@melainedcruze

Eating an apple will make you feel more AWAKE
VS.
in the morning than drinking a cup of coffee will.
@melainedcruze

ILLUSTRATE A FUN FACT

A BABY OYSTER
YOU WERE SPAT OUT
@melainedcruze
IS CALLED A SPAT

The dot over the letter i

I AM THE
TITTLE

is called the TITTLE
@melainedcruze

THE TEMPERATURE ON THE MOON CAN DROP BY UP TO 260°C (500°F) AT NIGHT.
WE ARE APPROACHING THE MOON. HOPE YOU'VE PACKED ENOUGH WOOLIES.
@melainedcruze

It is impossible to cry in
SPACE
I HAVE TO DEAL WITH THE GRAVITY OF THE SITUATION!
because of the lack of
GRAVITY
@melainedcruze

WHITE LIGHT is a mixture of all the colours in the SPECTRUM
@melainedcruze

ILLUSTRATE A FUN FACT
@melainedcruze

The first
E-MAIL
was sent in
1972
@melainedcruze

THE WORD
'TAXI'
is spelled the same in ENGLISH,
GERMAN, FRENCH, SWEDISH and
PORTUGUESE.
@melainedcruze

THE WORD DIASTIMA
MEANS HAVING A GAP
BETWEEN YOUR TEETH
@melainedcruze

Some forms of primitive life can survive anywhere that WATER is found, even in BOILING WATER or ICE.
@melainedcruze
UH... OH...!!
NO ONE WILL DRINK ME NOW!

There are about 1800 THUNDERSTORMS occuring on E🌀RTH at any given time.
HAPPENING RIGHT NOW !!!
@melainedcruze

ILLUSTRATE A FUN FACT

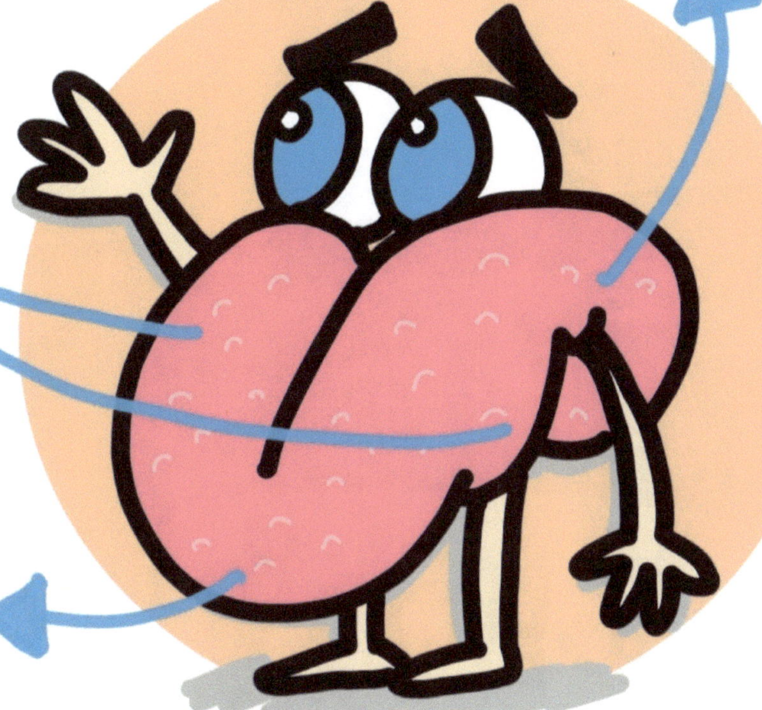

There are four
BASIC TASTES
BITTER
SOUR
SALTY &
SWEET
@melainedcruze
the HUMAN TONGUE can detect

BLACK PEPPER
is the most POPULAR spice in the WORLD
ACHOO!
@melainedcruze

90% of all extinct species

ARE BIRDS

In Ancient Egypt men & women wore EYESHADOW made from CRUSHED BEETLE
@melainedcruze

The world's oldest toy is
THE DOLL
I AM 3000 YEARS OLD!
Made in Greece
@melainedcruze

ILLUSTRATE A FUN FACT

EVERY
5
SECONDS
A BABY IS BORN
@melainedcruze

THOMAS EDISON was afraid of the DARK!
@melainedcruze

@melairedcruze

RECYCLING 1 GLASS JAR

=

saves enough ENERGY

to power a TELEVISION for 3 HOURS !

A
Dragonfly
LIVES
FOR ONLY
ONE DAY
@melainedcruze

ALLIGATORS HAVE 80 TEETH
ALL THE BETTER TO EAT YOU WITH!
@melainedcruze

ILLUSTRATE A FUN FACT

EVERY YEAR 4000 PEOPLE INJURE THEMSELVES WITH TEAPOTS

@melainedcruze

One in five children in the world
SCHOOL
has never been inside a school.
@melainedcruze

DIAMONDS ARE FLAMMABLE
YOU SET MY ♥ ON FIRE BABY!
@melainedcruze

YOUR EYES USE
25%
OF YOUR BRAIN'S POWER
@melainedcruze

←JUPITER is bigger than all the other planets in our SOLAR SYSTEM

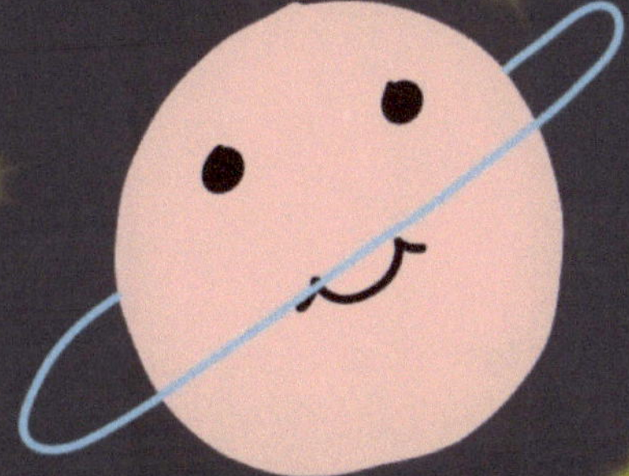

COMBINED
@melainedcruze

ILLUSTRATE A FUN FACT
@melainedcruze

You breathe
IN
and
OUT
about
23,000
times
in a day
@melainedcruze

Z
Z
Z
Z
Z
A SNAIL CAN
SLEEP FOR THREE
YEARS
@melainedcruze

A BEAVER CAN HOLD IT'S BREATH FOR UPTO 45 MINUTES UNDERWATER
@melainedcruze

ICEBERGS have been fitted with sailing gear & sailed for 2400 miles.
@melainedcruze

UH OH!...
BIG BEN, a clock in London, once lost time when a group of BIRDS used the minute hand as a PERCH!
@melainedcruze

ILLUSTRATE A FUN FACT

@melainedcruze

ILLUSTRATE A FUN FACT

ILLUSTRATE A FUN FACT

@melainedcruze

ILLUSTRATE A FUN FACT

@melainedcruze

ILLUSTRATE A FUN FACT

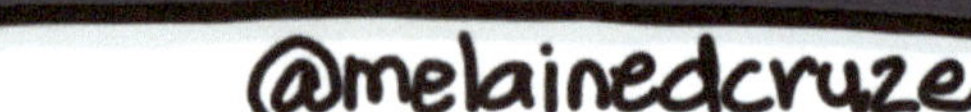

ABOUT THE AUTHOR

Melaine is a mom, musician, song bird, artist, illustrator, visual thinker, innovation strategist, lifelong learner…
See more of her work @melainedcruze

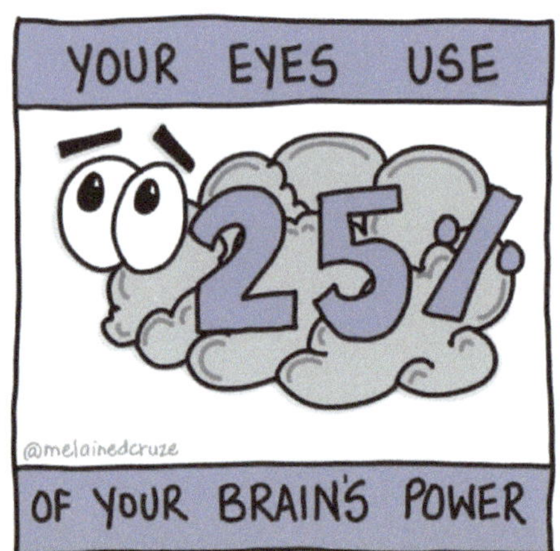

A FUN FACT-FILLED BOOK

Ideal for your coffee table, desk, car trips, travel, while waiting for food to arrive at the restaurant, in the doctor's waiting room...

Includes bonus pages to draw your own facts!